AGLAIA KREMEZI

Meze

Tapas and Antipasti

Photography by SIMON WHEELER

THE MASTER CHEFS

TED SMART

AGLAIA KREMEZI is a journalist and photographer with a regular column in the Athens Sunday newspaper *Kyriakatiki Eleftherotypia*. She also contributes to the *Los Angeles Times*.

Born in Athens, she has always been passionate about cooking and collects cookbooks and recipes from all over the world. She has studied the history of Greek and Mediterranean food in detail and has taken part in conferences on food in several countries.

Her book, *The Foods of Greece*, published in the USA in 1993, won a Julia Child Award for first cookbook. A compilation of her food columns, *Recipes and Stories* (1993), became a best-seller in Greece and was followed by a second collection entitled *Garlic, Honey and Mandrake*. She has written two other cookbooks in English: *Mediterranean Pantry* (1994) and *Mediterranean Hot* (1996).

CONTENTS

And while you are drinking, let these tasty dishes be brought to you: the belly of a sow in cumin and sharp vinegar and silphium; the tender race of roasted birds, whatever may be in season. Have nothing to do with those Syracusans who drink only in the manner of frogs and eat nothing.

ARCHESTRATUS, 4TH CENTURY BC
(translated by J. Wilkins and S. Hill, Prospect Books)

INTRODUCTION

The essence of the Mediterranean way of eating is the assortment of little dishes known variously as meze, tapas or antipasti. Far more than just the prelude to a meal, these little dishes can easily be a substitute for lunch or dinner, creating a leisurely feast, always accompanied by wine or something stronger. Everybody can help themselves from the sharing table, using forks for some dishes, fingers for others.

It was difficult to select just ten recipes from the many popular and much-loved Mediterranean meze. I went back and forth, having second thoughts, especially about stuffed vine leaves. Finally I decided to include the simplest dishes which, in addition to being delicious, would be easy to prepare, even by a first-time cook, and which used readily available ingredients. I also chose recipes that could be made ahead of time, so that the cook can relax with the guests.

Aglaie

GREEN OLIVES WITH CORIANDER,
lemon, orange and garlic

600 G/1¼ LB GREEN OLIVES IN
    BRINE, DRAINED
3 TABLESPOONS CORIANDER SEEDS,
    COARSELY CRUSHED
1 LEMON, CUT IN THIN SLICES
PARED ZEST OF 1 ORANGE
2 GARLIC CLOVES, SLICED
2–4 SPRIGS OF THYME
1 FRESH RED CHILLI, SLIT
    LENGTHWAYS AND SEEDED
    (OPTIONAL)
5 TABLESPOONS LEMON JUICE
3 TABLESPOONS ORANGE JUICE
ABOUT 375 ML/12 FL OZ FRUITY
    OLIVE OIL

MAKES 1 LITRE/1¾ PINTS

Taste one or two of the olives. If they are very salty, rinse in lukewarm water and dry on paper towels. Place the olives in a bowl, add the coriander, lemon slices, orange zest and garlic and toss to mix thoroughly.

Transfer the olives to a large jar and add the thyme, and the chilli, if you are using it. Beat the lemon and orange juice together with the olive oil and pour over the olives to cover them. Cover the jar and keep at room temperature for 1 day, shaking often. Store in the refrigerator for up to 1 month.

An hour or two before you want to eat them, bring the olives to room temperature. Serve with crusty bread and young, fresh, unsalted cheese, such as a French goats' cheese, Greek manouri or Italian ricotta.

YOGURT CHEESE WITH HERBS
and garlic

600 G/1¼ LB GREEK STRAINED
   YOGURT
1–2 GARLIC CLOVES, FINELY
   CHOPPED
1½ TEASPOONS SEA SALT
½–1½ TEASPOONS GROUND WHITE
   PEPPER
3 BUNCHES OF DILL, CHOPPED
6 SPRIGS OF CORIANDER,
   CHOPPED
7 SPRIGS OF FLAT-LEAF PARSLEY,
   CHOPPED

SERVES 8–10

Put all the ingredients into a bowl
and stir well to mix. (You can vary
the herbs according to taste or
availability. For example you can
use only dill, or you can substitute
parsley for the dill and
complement it with mint or basil.)

Line another bowl with a
double layer of muslin or a linen
tea towel and pour in the yogurt
mixture. Gather the ends of the
cloth and tie them together with a
piece of kitchen string, making a
loop so you can hang it from a
large wooden spoon, keeping it
well clear of the bottom of the
bowl. Leave to drain for 8–12
hours or overnight.

Untie the cloth and remove the
soft cheese. Serve with fresh bread,
crostini (page 29) or crackers.

This will keep for about 1
week in the refrigerator, in a
covered bowl.

BRUSCHETTA WITH HERBS,
anchovies and peppers

12 SPRIGS OF FLAT-LEAF PARSLEY
6–8 LARGE BASIL LEAVES
4 SPRIGS OF DILL
1 GARLIC CLOVE
4 ANCHOVY FILLETS
2 TABLESPOONS CAPERS, RINSED
    AND DRAINED
1 TEASPOON BALSAMIC VINEGAR
4 TABLESPOONS FRUITY
    OLIVE OIL
CAYENNE PEPPER
2 LARGE RED PEPPERS, GRILLED
    (PAGE 30)
6 BRUSCHETTA SLICES (PAGE 29)

SERVES 6

Put the parsley, basil, dill, garlic, anchovies and 1 tablespoon of the capers into a food processor or blender and process to make a smooth paste. Add the vinegar, olive oil and cayenne pepper to taste and process for a few more seconds. Leave to stand.

Cut the grilled red peppers into thin strips.

Just before serving, make the bruschetta. Spread the herb and anchovy mixture on the warm bruschetta and top with red pepper strips and whole capers.

SMOKED FISH SPREAD

ABOUT 200 G/7 OZ SKINNED AND
    BONED SMOKED FISH (KIPPER,
    SMOKED MACKEREL OR
    SMOKED HADDOCK)
4 SPRING ONIONS, MAINLY WHITE
    PART, ROUGHLY CHOPPED
1 TABLESPOON RED WINE VINEGAR
    OR SHERRY VINEGAR
4–6 TABLESPOONS LEMON JUICE
2–3 POTATOES (300–400 G/
    11–14 OZ), BOILED AND PEELED
125 ML/4 FL OZ OLIVE OIL
FLAT-LEAF PARSLEY, TO GARNISH

SERVES 10–12

Place the smoked fish, spring onions, vinegar and 3 tablespoons of the lemon juice in a food processor and pulse to make a purée. Add 1–2 potatoes and, with the machine running, pour in the olive oil through the funnel. Blend for a few seconds to get a smooth purée. Taste and adjust the flavour with more lemon juice or more potato as required.

Cover and refrigerate for at least 3 hours or overnight.

Garnish with parsley and serve with fresh bread or crostini (page 29), or as a dip with crudités.

AUBERGINE DIP WITH WALNUTS

2 LARGE AUBERGINES, ABOUT
    450 G/1 LB EACH
2 TABLESPOONS OLIVE OIL
½–1 FRESH RED CHILLI, SEEDED
    AND FINELY CHOPPED
125 G/4 OZ WALNUTS
1 LARGE GARLIC CLOVE, FINELY
    CHOPPED
2–3 TABLESPOONS SHERRY VINEGAR
3–4 TABLESPOONS EXTRA VIRGIN
    OLIVE OIL
½ TEASPOON SEA SALT

SERVES 10–12

Place the aubergines under a very
hot grill, letting the skin blacken
and blister to give the aubergines a
smoky flavour. Turn from time to
time to cook on all sides; this will
take about 40 minutes.

Peel off the skins, cut the
aubergines in half lengthways and
scoop out the flesh. Leave the flesh
in a colander to drain for at least
30 minutes.

Meanwhile, heat the olive oil in
a small frying pan and sauté the
chilli until soft, about 2 minutes.

Place the drained aubergines,
the fried chilli with its oil, the
walnuts, garlic, 2 tablespoons of the
vinegar, 3 tablespoons of the extra
virgin olive oil and the salt in a
food processor and pulse to make a
smooth paste. Taste and add more
vinegar, oil or salt if required.

Serve as a dip with crudités or
with fresh bread, crostini,
bruschetta (page 29) or crackers.

This will keep for about 1
week in the refrigerator, in a
covered bowl.

SPICY FETA AND PEPPER SPREAD

3 TABLESPOONS OLIVE OIL

1 LARGE RED PEPPER, SEEDED AND
     COARSELY CHOPPED

1 SMALL FRESH RED CHILLI, SEEDED
     AND CHOPPED, OR
     ½–1 TEASPOON CAYENNE PEPPER

450 G/1 LB FETA CHEESE, OR
     300 G/11 OZ FETA CHEESE AND
     150 G/5 OZ COTTAGE CHEESE

SERVES 10–12

Heat the olive oil in a frying pan and sauté the pepper together with the chilli, if you are using it, until soft, about 5 minutes. If you are using cayenne pepper, add it to the pan a few seconds before removing it from the heat.

Taste the feta and if it is very salty, rinse in cold water. Crumble it with a fork and place it in a food processor. Add the sautéed peppers and their oil and pulse to make a smooth paste.

Serve with fresh bread, crostini (page 29) or crackers.

This will keep for about 1 week in the refrigerator, in a covered bowl. Bring to room temperature before serving.

SPINACH AND YOGURT CROSTINI
with pine nuts

675 G/1½ LB SPINACH LEAVES,
    WASHED WELL AND COARSELY
    CHOPPED
1 BUNCH OF FLAT-LEAF PARSLEY,
    CHOPPED
600 G/1¼ LB GREEK STRAINED
    YOGURT
2 GARLIC CLOVES, FINELY CHOPPED
½–1 FRESH CHILLI, FINELY
    CHOPPED
SALT AND FRESHLY GROUND BLACK
    PEPPER
40 G/1½ OZ PINE NUTS, TOASTED
CROSTINI (PAGE 29)

SERVES 10–12

Place the spinach in a pan with only the water left on the leaves after washing. Place the pan over high heat, cover and let the spinach wilt; this will take about 2–3 minutes, but remember to toss the pan once or twice and be careful not to let the spinach burn. Tip the wilted spinach into a colander and leave to drain. When the spinach is cool enough to handle, squeeze out as much liquid as possible, then chop finely.

Put the spinach in a bowl with the parsley, yogurt, garlic and chilli, and stir well to mix. Season to taste. Cover and refrigerate for at least 3 hours or overnight.

To serve, spread the spinach mixture thickly on the crostini and sprinkle with pine nuts.

The mixture will keep for about 4 days in the refrigerator, in a covered bowl.

TORTILLA
(Potato and onion omelette)

4 TABLESPOONS OLIVE OIL

1 KG/2¼ LB LARGE POTATOES,
   PEELED, CUT IN HALF
   LENGTHWAYS AND SLICED

3 ONIONS, DICED

1 GREEN PEPPER, DICED

5 EGGS, BEATEN

SALT AND FRESHLY GROUND BLACK
   PEPPER

SERVES 8

Heat the oil in a nonstick frying pan and sauté the potatoes, onions and pepper for a few minutes, stirring frequently. Cover and cook over medium heat for 10–15 minutes, stirring occasionally, until tender. Drain in a colander, then return to the frying pan.

Season the eggs generously with salt and pepper, then pour the eggs over the vegetables and cook over low heat, shaking the pan often, until the omelette no longer sticks to the sides of the pan.

Place a large plate over the omelette and invert the frying pan. Slide the omelette back into the pan and cook for another minute or so. Transfer to a plate, cut into squares and serve warm or at room temperature, by itself or on crostini (page 29).

GAMBAS AL AJILLO
(Garlic prawns)

ABOUT 5 TABLESPOONS OLIVE OIL

450 G/1 LB UNCOOKED PRAWNS,
SHELLED, WITH TAILS LEFT ON

4 GARLIC CLOVES, SLICED

½–1 RED FRESH CHILLI, SEEDED
AND FINELY CHOPPED
(OPTIONAL)

SALT AND FRESHLY GROUND BLACK
PEPPER

3 TABLESPOONS CHOPPED PARSLEY

SERVES 6–8

Heat the olive oil in a heavy frying pan or flameproof dish and add the prawns, garlic and chilli, if you are using it. Cook, stirring with a spatula, for about 3 minutes, until the prawns are firm. Sprinkle with salt, pepper and parsley and serve at once while the prawns are still sizzling, accompanied by crusty bread to dip into the sauce.

VARIATION

You can substitute boned cubed chicken (breast or thigh) for the prawns. It needs to cook for about 10 minutes, so add the garlic and chilli after 6 minutes.

CHEESE AND SPINACH TRIANGLES
with leek and fennel

ABOUT 125 ML/4 FL OZ OLIVE OIL

1 LEEK, THINLY SLICED

1 FENNEL BULB, FINELY CHOPPED

225 G/8 OZ FROZEN SPINACH,
    CHOPPED

1 BUNCH OF PARSLEY, CHOPPED

85 G/3 OZ PECORINO OR FETA
    CHEESE, GRATED

85 G/3 OZ PARMESAN OR MATURE
    CHEDDAR CHEESE, GRATED

1 EGG

SALT AND FRESHLY GROUND BLACK
    PEPPER

14 FILO PASTRY SHEETS

MAKES 28

Preheat the oven to 200°C/400°F/
Gas Mark 6.

Heat 3 tablespoons of the olive
oil in a frying pan and sauté the
leek and fennel until tender, about
8 minutes. Add the spinach and
parsley and sauté, stirring, until dry.
Remove from the heat, stir in the
cheeses and egg; season to taste.

Work with one sheet of filo
pastry at a time, keeping the rest
covered with a damp tea towel to
prevent it from drying out. Lightly
brush a sheet of filo with olive oil
and fold it in half lengthways.
Brush the top with oil and cut it
into two strips. Place 1 heaped
tablespoon of the spinach mixture
at the end of a strip of filo and fold
up to make a triangular parcel
(page 28). Brush with a little more
oil and place on an oiled baking
sheet. Repeat to make 28 parcels.

Bake for about 35 minutes,
until golden brown. Serve warm or
at room temperature.

If fresh (not frozen) filo pastry
is used, the uncooked parcels can
be frozen; cook from frozen.

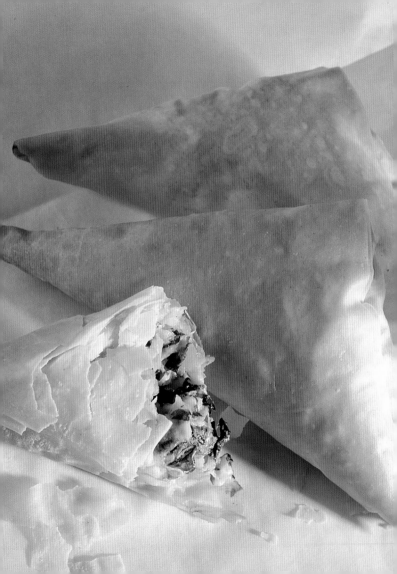

THE BASICS

FOLDING FILO PASTRY TRIANGLES

1 Place a heaped tablespoon of filling at the end of a strip of filo pastry.

2 Fold the corner of the pastry over the filling to reach the other edge, making a triangle.

3 Fold the triangle up over the pastry strip.

4 Continue folding the triangle across and up until all the pastry is folded around the filling.

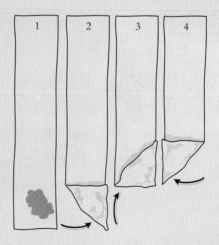

BREAD

The many Mediterranean dips and spreads may be served with raw vegetables – courgettes, carrots, fennel, spring onions, celery, red or green peppers – but bread is always on the table. As an alternative to fresh bread, try making crisp crostini or garlic-scented bruschetta.

CROSTINI

Preheat the oven to 200°C/400°F/Gas Mark 6.

Cut a baguette diagonally into 1 cm/½ inch thick slices. Brush on both sides with good-quality olive oil and bake in the hot oven for about 10 minutes or until lightly browned, turning once.

Crostini can be made 2–3 days in advance; they should be stored in an airtight container.

BRUSCHETTA

Use Italian country-style bread, cut into 1 cm/½ inch thick slices and then halved. Cut 1–2 garlic cloves in half. Grill the bread on both sides and rub the warm bread with the garlic, then drizzle with fruity extra virgin olive oil. Serve warm or at room temperature.

Bruschetta can simply be sprinkled with salt and fresh oregano, or topped with thin slices of ripe tomato or fresh cheese.

GRILLED PEPPERS

When grilled, red and yellow peppers become soft and sweet – ideal as a colourful and healthy addition to crostini or bruschetta, and also delicious as a salad in their own right, perhaps with a few black olives, anchovies and basil leaves.

Wash and dry the peppers. Cut them into quarters lengthways, discarding the stems and seeds.

Line a grill rack with foil and arrange the pepper pieces on it, skin side up. Place the rack about 8 cm/3 inches away from the grill and cook the peppers until their skin is black and blistered, 3–4 minutes.

Place the peppers in a plastic bag or in a bowl and cover. Leave for 10 minutes, then peel (the skin of the peppers will come off very easily).

The grilled peppers can be kept in a vinaigrette dressing for about 1 week in the refrigerator, in a covered bowl.

THE MASTER CHEFS

SOUPS
ARABELLA BOXER

MEZE, TAPAS AND ANTIPASTI
AGLAIA KREMEZI

PASTA SAUCES
GORDON RAMSAY

RISOTTO
MICHELE SCICOLONE

SALADS
CLARE CONNERY

MEDITERRANEAN
ANTONY WORRALL THOMPSON

VEGETABLES
PAUL GAYLER

LUNCHES
ALASTAIR LITTLE

COOKING FOR TWO
RICHARD OLNEY

FISH
RICK STEIN

CHICKEN
BRUNO LOUBET

SUPPERS
VALENTINA HARRIS

THE MAIN COURSE
ROGER VERGÉ

ROASTS
JANEEN SARLIN

WILD FOOD
ROWLEY LEIGH

PACIFIC
JILL DUPLEIX

CURRIES
PAT CHAPMAN

HOT AND SPICY
PAUL AND JEANNE RANKIN

THAI
JACKI PASSMORE

CHINESE
YAN-KIT SO

VEGETARIAN
KAREN LEE

DESSERTS
MICHEL ROUX

CAKES
CAROLE WALTER

COOKIES
ELINOR KLIVANS

THE MASTER CHEFS

This edition produced for The Book People Ltd,

Hall Wood Avenue, Haydock, St Helens WA11 9UL

Text © copyright 1996 Aglaia Kremezi

Photographs © copyright 1996 Simon Wheeler

First published in 1996 by

WEIDENFELD & NICOLSON

THE ORION PUBLISHING GROUP

ORION HOUSE

5 UPPER ST MARTIN'S LANE

LONDON WC2H 9EA

British Library Cataloguing-in-Publication data
A catalogue record for this book is available
from the British Library.

ISBN 0 297 83630 7

DESIGNED BY THE SENATE
EDITOR MAGGIE RAMSAY
FOOD STYLIST JOY DAVIES